THE HAPPIEST DAY OF MY LIFE

▼

Kevin Burris

FUTURECYCLE PRESS

www.futurecycle.org

Library of Congress Control Number: 2016943371

Published by FutureCycle Press
Lexington, Kentucky, USA

ISBN 978-1-942371-06-9

For my parents

Contents

I

II

I

Daffodils

We have thrown off the snow, spiked
revolution through the frozen heart
of a czar who knows no color.

We have come for him—
Hades at his Stygian palace.
Yellow torches in the courtyard

announce our new democracy.
We have voted in the sun, a tide
of tulips rising behind us.

Balance

The dog walks by with an octopus
toy in her mouth. May Day,

first of the month. Outside the trees
can't imagine any more green.

Everything is as it should be
for once. Not a misplaced mote

of dust in this sunbeam.
My therapist and I will have nothing

to talk about. I place Carl Jung
and his purposeful work on my shelf

and sip the scented tea of contentment.
If there is another life,

some spiritual counterweight to this
Zen of the moment, I must

also be sitting there, steam rising
from a cup this close to overflowing.

Napping

Summer afternoons when that dog isn't barking
in the distance, where we might hear him
because the windows are wide open,
and leaves on the lilac bush have begun to wilt
for lack of rain and the sun bears straight down
upon them, and every living thing is hiding
in the moist woodwork of our old house,
we at three in the afternoon are sleeping
certainly, in our bed, satisfied
that the overhead fan with one bent blade
counts every single second sneaking past.

Between Storms

Grass gets cut and weeds
plucked. A spot of paint is laid
on a shutter. Fresh wax

coats the backs of cars.
Woodchucks trust just enough
to nose from root-rimmed holes.

Crows shop the stream bed's edge
for snacks. Squirrels scratch
and preen on dripping branches.

Seeds flutter, fly, parachute, glide.
Black clouds scuffle and fight,
argue with light. Crackling,

blue-white as a bolt shatters,
push comes once more to shove.
Leaves begin to chatter.

You lift your cheek from mine
for a moment, as if to answer,
and the rain, again, says *hush*.

Before the Poem

There is the relief of the page,
the wilderness of it, the frontier,
the promise not to judge.
There is the wink of it, the nudge,
the open water, oceanic.
There is the harbor of it,
the welcoming, the carpet
untrudged by muddy feet.
There is the cry of it, the need,
the heel and leg and curve,
the jounce and jangle then
the buy your friends a shot.
There is the campfire of it,
the stars and rising moon,
the baby in the crib of it,
the June, the nest at noon
beneath a veil of tilting leaves.
There is the home of it at last,
the car in the drive,
the key in the door,
the face you love, returning.

The Happiest Day of My Life

Monet might capture the dawn,
the raw truth of a beginning, softened
with pastel colors. I favor oranges and
of course he would too.

Breakfast is light on the veranda—
an ocean view, the surf up, maybe
a volcano, snow-peaked, to the right
behind a pitcher of fresh-squeezed juice.

There would be no schedule, no weight
of the full day ahead, just a quiet
certainty of things and you
catching the breeze in your hair.

I suppose I could own a Ferrari,
but not today. Today would be
too fragile, not a thing for machines,
not a place for noise or speed. Today

would be its own machine, well-oiled,
gliding on an unseen track,
something Newton might smile at
sitting in his perfumed apple grove.

I'd be halfway through the best book
ever written while someone French
conjured lunch in the cooking-show kitchen.
I think I hear a robin singing.

The family will send cards again—
no particular occasion, a little something
to let me know how much they care, each
leavened with a wry personal note.

There would be some mention,
there would have to be, with a laugh,
of the worst day of my life, some passing
reference, counterpoint to jazz

playing low in the background, a band
I'll see tonight, front row at Montreux,
that perfect quintet at the top of their game,
sculpting song from starlight.

Afternoon will call for sailboats—
gulls gliding on a single white wing—
above a blue Homer once named Aegyptus,
a reflection

of the sky today, limitless, so deep,
I know if I tilt my head and look,
I will meet the eyes of Aphrodite
and I will find no end in them.

Old Movies

In the movie that tells a story of the past,
a man in a fedora looks you right in the eye.
He smokes as he talks in Tommy gun bursts.
At ringside, in a nightclub, on the docks,
he means business.

The woman beneath her velvet cloche
will cut you down to size with a glance.
She draws her words like thread
through a button and ties them off
in tight, sure knots.

If they kiss, this man and woman—
after she has slapped him, after he
has held her helpless—they kiss
long and hard as if they might never
see each other again,

as if they know we are watching,
each in our own comfortable darkness,
longing to see how things were certain
once, before we were born
hatless, into a wilderness of color.

Rainy Sidewalks by the Seine

Whatshername? Claudine Longet? Chanteuse
who shot a ski bum in the stomach. Wife
of Andy Williams, used to coo
rainy sidewalks by the Seine. Your co-
host of the Andy Williams Christmas Special:
artist, mother, adulteress, murderer.
I'd like to draw one drop from that dark well:
those rainy sidewalks by the river, cobblestones
I've never seen, the streets of Paris.
I don't even know if they exist outside
her musing contralto. But here they are again,
soaked in a mist of jazz guitar.
A little Mingus moving on bass.
I see raindrops on new black leather—
her shoes as she walks—the surging
surface of the water, a slow steady scat,
wrought iron, not too much color in the grass.
It's early May and the world is a broken heart.
Ex-con now or dead, she is forever
far from miniskirts, Santa Claus, the soft spring
rain she sang, the sidewalks, the Seine.

Live at the Blue Note

Stalking heat like a bride
of Dracula, she flutters
on a jazz-blue breeze,
blonde and bumptious,
up to the porch light tap.

In a swarm of suburb's
sons, she is queen,
slinging smiles and D-cups
like eggs
at a hash-house breakfast bar.

She lights a cigar,
her languid hips drifting
sweet as Cuban smoke
past the saxophone's note.
Coochie Coochie Carmen

Miranda blows a kiss
behind her longneck beer,
where her fingers tease and peel
a label like a tongue.
As the band cooks

night into promises
of maybe and maybe not,
she starts fires with a wink
and burns down every house
on Green Dolphin Street.

Discipline

I am not too old to remember
the little engine that could, steaming
down his track, little engine brow
furrowed with determination,

and the voice of my mother
exalting his redemption
or in the kitchen singing
Just what makes that little old ant...

Yes, you can, she would say
to the boy who could not,
would not button his obstinate
Salvation Army coat

or wake as an acolyte
to ascend an ancient Schwinn
four miles toward the sunrise
of six o'clock mass,

who could not will himself
to walk the last lonely block
of December's endless paper route.
I cannot be old enough

to forget rich days unwasted,
the music of muscle well-toned,
my steady gait, a certain pace,
the breath I share
with the wind at my back.

Madagascar

It lies somewhere in the mist
of an eighth-grade geography quiz,
disappearing but distinct, it is still

exotic as a flower on the moon,
a shadow anchored
in an alien ocean, a lemur
on a leash, a stepping stone

to India and Bali, to Singapore,
to Malay pirates east of Java,
knives in their teeth, backlit
by the fires of Krakatoa.

Antananarivo, Antsiranana:
these are the names of its places.
If you find it at all, you will find it to the right

of Zanzibar and Dar es Salaam,
Tarzan's treehouse, the lost lake
of an English queen, the mines
of King Solomon.

But you will never find it
(and neither could I)
beside a certain number,
the very last question once
between me and a carefree summer.

The Cloud Factory

Even now I see a billow rising,
frost-white beard on a blue summer sky,
the stack shadow's black casting
a pencil line across a country mile.

And my mother's conspiratorial smile
as Dad, from the old Dodge's cockpit,
on our yearly vacation trek North,
pointed out the sights of Wisconsin—

where Daniel Boone met Father Marquette,
where cavemen left the last dinosaur dead.
Where—in the distance, in that Battersea station—
I could see from my comics-strewn seat

men of science in starched white lab coats
manufacture clouds and set them free.
In polished steel vats they'd mix secret potions—
a pinch of Barsoom, the breath of a bat—

and out from the lip of that great painted stack
dragons would rise, a swan or a bear,
a six-masted schooner set sail in the air,
or the face of a child, familiar, unexpected,
captured in glass, awe in his reflection.

June Bugs

Deep in chitinous armor, ardor
for the heavenly promise of light
hooks them. Racked by the night
in windows they hang and suffer.

Rattle and rage—the vain frustration
of carapace and mandible. Six
strong legs locked, feet like picks
search a screen's combination.

At patio doors, hour upon hour
they trade their wings for lust.
Falling, could lost angels buzz
more fury at Oblivion's power

which lays them down so soon,
earthbound, for loving the moon?

Among the Eloi

Here in the moment
all things are possible.

I can hear the thin voice of a bluebird
warble its best piccolo.

I can see the sunset from Mykonos
or feel the slow waltz of continents.

There is time enough for everything here,
time for the long, easy conversation

I never had with my father,
time for the celebratory beer with Mom

after the last out in the last game
of the Cubs' World Series victory.

There is time for that fat, flat maple leaf
cartwheeling through rush hour

and time for me, nested here
in the tall tree of Sunday's standard coffee shop,

the view from my window
infinite as a sunny day.

Two Pots of Begonias

The house is a shamble tucked
in shadows. Deep green
menace, elms bending low
turn their leaves dark like
holes in the air.

One bottom-loose shutter hangs,
top tilted and raised,
an eyebrow arched as if
to ask: *What are you doing
here, at this door?*

Rusting blood from the railings
on the cocked concrete stoop,
steps down to a sidewalk, crooked
brook that tumbles to join
the asphalt floes of a broken drive.

That impudent river, stuck
out like a tongue from the tumbledown
garage, from a shattered Ford,
drains down to the street,
to gridlocked cars in the heat.

But there at the end, set
against this brooding traffic snarl,
against the tin drum din of the radio's world,
two pots of begonias beam
and stem the tide of all the rest.

II

You Bring Pumpkins to Carve

Day's end,
I turn back my clock,
have darkness for supper.

On the phone you are bright,
sudden
as a summer penny.

I wash dishes then,
wipe down the walnut table,
wrap it in news

of your arrival, bent
with what might steal a sinful
smile or hatch a bird of prey.

And in the orbit of an eye,
in the joyous
journey round a wind-swept stem,

I understand again
this carving, this design,
your careful hand guiding mine.

Nocturne

Only at night, only
when shadows damask
the lunar contours
of your back and shoulders,

when you speak in dreams
of bumblebees and harvest light
and sink back, brave
explorer to the quicksand lands

beneath your quilted comforter,
then the night birds trill,
then the scent of jasmine
answers with perfect clarity.

October

for Katie

The shadow of a honeybee
on a half-drawn window shade
writes the word *honeybee*
across this sun-starved page.

Passing conversation,
a secret whispered by a breeze
to two neighboring Acacias,
is gold among their leaves.

Gilded sunlight stretching west
in a languorous adieu
waves every color to come rest
here, with you.

You were born to gold and grace.
You married gratitude and gave him faith.

Thirty-four Cranes

Look to Rilke for help
to measure their significance.
He could see as you do now,

in the dusk. He would tell you
to see them only, white
runes from a feathered moon

meant for you at this moment.
Trust, and read each one
perched here in the rib cage

of a marsh. All that is left of light
circles and saves itself,
keeps its own company.

Mourning Dove

A song like the wind on its hinge
slowly swinging
ushers us into our days.

We groom our hair,
brush teeth,
test memories in the mirror.

We make lists,
gather the hours ahead like stones,
and carry them in our pockets.

Because we feel this weight,
because we know gravity
as the urge to fly,

sometimes at sunrise
we close our eyes
and listen.

Miss You

I saw a Scarlet Tanager and I thought of you,
the way your brow lifts and your eyes
cloud with dreams when you watch a bird.

It was branch-hopping from spot to spot
of sun on young maple leaves—
impossible red against impossible green,

May splashing, both feet in a puddle
of luminescence. I saw your face then,
color of a new moon, a whisper-blue

reflection in my window, a hint
of you, soft and cool, taking wing.

Twelfth Moon

She strikes conversation
in hallway mirrors,
describes her face to the night,
to snow-covered rooftops
eavesdropping ice.

She glides
dark stairs down
from a sacred height,
bathes in bone-white light,
the latticed cage of a window.

She slips inside
to bloom behind closed eyes
as a lotus blooms, pale, serene,
undisturbed on the surface
of moonlit waters.

Disconnect

The phone is mute; no magnetic
word swims in its memory.

I cannot find the hat I wore
when we dropped the top and drove

four hours into the west.
Our connections were made

and broken by a bolt of anger.
There was not supposed to be a storm

for a thousand weekend miles
or clouds going gangrene

so suddenly we buttoned up
in a Citgo, wind keening like a dial tone.

Hephaestus at the Weekend

He scrubs his nails with ash. The earth they hold
counts ten degrees of honor for those scarred
hands with which he moves the forged colossus,
grips the chains of overhead cranes, cuts cores
and cavities; the tribute, polished and annealed,
that every day the gods demand from steel.

In leather apron, goggles, and tattoos he's bent
beneath the busty pinups at his bench.
Dactyl, demon, maker of thunderbolts,
he pushes ancient carts on concrete floors,
tends a fire of EDM sparks, the laser's hearth.
In acid baths he'll etch a clutch of roses.

At dawn he stops to clip a fresh cigar,
then hitches his old Harley to the morning star.

Where the Mouse Was

White tile gleams, scrubbed clean
by daylight, bleach, and paper towel.
No vestige remains, no whisker or tooth.

Its legs were splayed, tiny toes
and fingers spread wide as eyes,
surprised when the hammer fell.

Black tail marked the kitchen floor,
its rigor exclaiming in sudden shout,
outrage, betrayal, disbelief—

I died for cheese! No more
midnight snacks by a cabinet's crack,
the nervous skirt of refrigerator door.

No menus left, no treasure maps
to cookie crumbs and popcorn kernels,
the fugitive grape that rolled

beneath a stove's squat black shadow.
No exits wait in baseboard corners.
Nothing will brave darkness tonight,

in the quietest hour, to pause and listen
for the faucet drip, the furnace grumble,
the ticking of the coiled clock.

Seriatim

I take no comfort in description,
in the tropic haze
of summer outside my window.

Wind blows; leaves yield
the muted shades of hidden life.
A steady stream of traffic passes.

Nothing starts, nothing stops.
Someone's exposed
the mechanism of a time machine.

I can see the continuous
in this creamy slant of light.
There are frictionless days

when we are borne dreaming
on our Procrustean beds
to the banks of a waiting river.

Ammonite

Ammon's crown,
were you once
the ocean's darling?

Did you whorl
a lifetime's treasure
in a chambered shell?

You drew circles
on a sea long since
turned to sand.

Curled in my hand,
your empty home
is cold, polished

pyrite by the look,
Greek root of fire,
a kind of gold.

Ageratum

These stones stop the day
where a May sun bleeds
colorless and cold on dusty grass.
Masks of the dead stand
gray-eyed and blind,
statues above an empty road.

Beside the towers of spent lives,
a courtyard where sleep rewards
priests; among the flags of warriors,
one tiny bloom burns,
set sapphire in these ruins
where you dwell, still.

Whose hands hold you
now, as they did a lifetime ago,
for one year and one month, only
to lose you and to keep you
here, with a seed of open sky
at your small bedside?

Such love you must know
carries your name
with a poor clay pot that shames
the great in their gilded tombs
and lights this dark garden
with a single ageless flame.

The Child, Embarrassed for His Parents

My father sang
at weddings, at wakes,
at the drop of a hat.

Pure Irish tenor poured
unbidden "Danny Boy"
into Waterford.

In his army days
(so the story goes)
men would hoist him,

a small man,
on a jeep
so his songs

would warm the trees
of the Ardennes,
the snow,

the hearts
of soldiers
far from home.

I would not listen
years later,
on Christmas nights,

after dinner's candlelight.
He was, I thought,
just way uncool.

My mother sneezed,
and when she sneezed,
would sneeze five times,

no less, no more.
Caught in some store,
mortified, after four

I was so
damned certain
she would not dare another

save for attention.
There was no room in me.
I was all judgment.

Now my father's voice,
colored whiskey,
is long decanted.

When last it poured,
it poured in sips
enough to taste,

to savor
the greater spirit
of his youth.

I warm my glass
with aging hands,
drink deep;

and if I sneeze,
I sneeze five times
for no good reason.

Building a Battleship

Wait for dusk, a safe two hours
after the workmen have gone.
Become your own shadow, there
beneath the searchlight glare
of mercury vapor light.

Steal among skeletons—
the no-man's-lands of new subdivisions—
fresh pine studs and beams,
one-by-twos, two-by-fours, a carpet of fallen nails.
Collect them in the basket of a bike,

as the boatman collects a passage. Bury them
beneath your father's basement workbench.
When the time is right, break his law—
touch his hand drill, his hammer, his hacksaw.
Hold them in your hands.

Choose your hull carefully, no knots, no warp,
the best unblemished board.
Lay a square along the center line.
Mark the spearhead bow, lock it
in the ancient vise, and cut.

Saw the gun deck and the bridge.
Nail four blocks of turrets one by one
to the main deck and into each
hammer galvanized three-penny teeth
of sixteen-inch guns.

Feel them watching from time to time
from the folds of battered black and white
Kodak prints, pinned
beneath the buzzing fluorescent light—
soldiers in the snow, posing,

a Thompson cradled in your father's arms.
Who are they? you once asked
in that innocence the time allowed.
He said little and nothing more:
Those boys are gone.

Add the deck rail's silver brads.
Trim them out with string.
Search out a dowel and slice it
for a funnel. Fix the stern
with a bent-nail seaplane crane.

Sweep the sawdust from the concrete floor.
Collect the cuttings. Tighten the vise.
Hang each tool in its sacred pegboard place.
Keep things where you put them. Put them away.
Carry your battleship into the day.

Breakfast Comes

Breakfast leaves untouched—
grape juice, one half
of a dry English muffin.

Down the hall, a man cries *water*.
Fox News, the Weather Channel
talk a hurricane toward the coast.

Doctor orders another day.
A new nurse adds her name
to the scheduled procession.

Check heart, pulse, kidneys, lungs,
turn him with the sun,
adjust his pillows.

The standard clock looks on
unblinking, past each hour
till breakfast comes.

At the River Saar

"While the fates permit, live happily..." —Seneca

They don't seem to notice me
standing here among them,
these three women in white.

We lean together
over a pool of black water
where a photograph floats.

It is a picture of you,
a soldier from History's book
of battles, the war of 1944,

and you are sitting in a Jeep
leaning toward the winter darkness
before you. There is a river

you are waiting to cross
with the small rubber boat behind you.
I wish I could touch your shoulder

and whisper the name of your wife,
the names of your children,
the promise of ten thousand days

when the sun will find you
once this night is past.
As one woman draws thread

from her spindle, one apportions it
with a smooth length of bone.
I wish you could know

what has been promised by the third,
to whom I quietly slipped a twenty,
the one with the shears in her hand.

Arboring

Oaks defy a cloudless sky.

Sister, stork-legged in tiger lilies,
     calls for rain.

Ten days in the nineties,
     even heat breathes slow.

Panama on the porch:
     Father in his favorite hat
         fishes for a cigarette,
            calls the dog.
Charlie

dreams a Labrador's dream,
     swims the lake at eight weeks.

Is this stillness now your voice?

On the water,
       mirrored heron
         listen twice.

Staggered, Stunned by Light

A week of rain, high water, night
cool enough still for sleep.
Beneath the surface, blue bruises
swim inside your skin.
You wait on whims
of territorial muskellunge
while you stare, dreaming.

Dreaming all the ages of your life,
your history is reduced
to one thin line extended
from the parchment of your hands,
a needle through the membrane
of Big Sand Lake.

Father, how does it come to this
last hour of our last day?
I can't see you for the light:
sudden sun, high and brutal,
shattered mirror of a bay, the white
relentlessness of gulls
circling for shore lunch scraps.

What They Know

Already geese know,
and owls, warning a harvest moon.

My breath knows, cocooned
in its new shadow.

Mud and straw know,
forsaking abandoned nests.

Dawn, I think, suspects
lead has entered blue veins.

Dreaming days,
poisoned in their wombs, know

what locusts rush to know
at turnstile spider webs.

Mice in baseboard beds
curled in dreams know, tremble

like the gallows basil,
its black leaves condemned.

Soon night will bend
close to keen on fallen snow

so the dead again may know
their true names.

Winter Storm

Grief is white and silent.
Skies bend close
enough to touch the forest-corpse

and gather as a prayer cap.
The weight of tears distilled
bows the sunflower's skull.

I follow a trail vanishing
between painted oaks,
a deer on the run.

My own footprints fill
behind me, and ahead
there is no way but snow.

Sunday

Worm-harvesting,
a dozen robins scour wet gravel:
the path through Pratt's Wayne Forest Preserve.
All the morning's thunder has been heard;
her storm's left to unravel.
Cupped leaves spill their winnings.

My dog's too lean
and, stiff with arthritis, he lags.
His tail droops in the heat.
He drags his feet.
Summer's cresting toward August.
There is corruption in green

Sumac and Solomon's Seal.
A single daylily leans
unwanted from a wall of weeds,
and now this family passes, fishermen
burdened with buckets, rods, and reels.
They seem grim as Bedouin

leaving an oasis.
Only their handicapped daughter speaks,
knows to speak, breaks our silence.
Pretty dog, she says in defiance
of whatever law won't let our eyes meet
or recall each other's faces.

One bright Sunday
when I was a child, my father whistled
in his best suit from our crushed stone driveway,
a cardinal's song after morning Mass.
I held my breath and listened
for answers from an elm's dark branches.

I'm listening still.
As milkweed ready their seed for flight,
I hear the cold that stars sing.
These fields will fill
with silence, deep woods rimed in moonlight.
I have spent my life expecting.

Nothing is here.
I've searched this sky too many seasons.
Perfect as a dream, certain as a mirror,
it reflects. There is no reason.
These black flies won't hesitate.
I don't know why I wait.

The dog's already fled,
hopscotching from patch to patch
of shade. He's slipped his collar,
spooked a rabbit he can't catch.
He kicks up dust ahead
and will not come when called.

III

The Grand Design

In this corner, Stephen Hawking,
physicist extraordinaire, Lucasian professor
of mathematics, cosmologist, and author
of *The Grand Design.*

He of the gravitational singularity,
the black hole, and a certain radiation
that bears his name.

Prisoner of his own body
who spans galaxies in his mind,
who counts infinities in this universe
and infinite others.

Who has seen at last no need
for any other author, no source or solace save
It is what it is.

And in this corner, Sasha,
sixty-five-pound female Malamute
who hates to be alone, who
one day, in my absence,
ate his book.

Join Me and We Can Rule the Universe

is one of my favorite movie lines.
It is always spoken by the most evil
personality in the universe: Emperor
of the Dark Side. Agent of Satan.
Brunette sorceress in a revealing
ruby-encrusted, golden-framework halter top.

Sometimes evil does not want the universe.
Sometimes a city will do, a small town,
or a single suburban home. If evil is having
a bad day, it may only want a truck or a car.
It might settle for a lawn ornament.

But if evil wants a city, that city
is always like New York—only darker—
with a fat, incompetent police chief
and an insane criminal kingpin, fireplug
of a thug with massive hands bunched
into fists, his expensive suit straining

at his shoulders, his bull neck. This guy
is a saint beside his girlfriend,
the fatal brunette in the form-fitting silk.
He isn't Ming, but he ought to be.
She isn't Circe, but she wants to be.

And though you and I and the audience
know evil does not need the help,
it can't resist making an offer
to the chiseled or statuesque champion
who has fallen under its power.

After a million times watching
the snake sell his apple, after the torture,
depravity, nakedness, fig leaves,
the march from the garden, the inevitability
of death, why do we still wait spellbound

while our hero tests his chains or throws
her defiant chin upward, prepared
to speak, we hope, with steely resolve
for all that is good in the world,
for what must certainly be right?

Man With a Funny Haircut

There is an Einstein in line
at the bank, hair like the bouquet
of important papers blooming
unexpectedly in his hands, petals falling,
as he searches for a pen.

In a rumpled suit, he is always
dryer-fresh, far from an iron
as a Scotsman, plaid and frowning
down the fairway from a par-five tee
beneath a storm of hair.

Rain-slicked, plastered, a valiant
Moe de cheveux in Bristol boots,
he stands alone at a bus stop,
six-foot-five, one hundred pounds
of haunted ostrich.

He won't see you watching. He'll turn
instead to his books and blueprints,
to the castle grounds inside his head
where winds freshen the pennants flying
high on sunlit turret tops.

All the Way to De Soto

I have driven three and a half hours
to hear a crow sing in the broken language
of Derrida and Foucault.

Here in the People's Free Space of Chicago,
where no money should ever change hands,
where poetry and sacks of flour
and hand-me-down jeans are free to all,
a bastard son of the Beats takes the stage.

It rains a lot in Oregon,
the state from which he hails, and to celebrate
he has chosen every shade of black as his companion.

When he is not brushing a gothic lock
of hair from his Poean brow, he assures us
there is wisdom here: lessons for the second wife,
indictments of the torturer.

But these are not the words he uses.
The words he uses have been shaken in a can
and spilled like a pair of dice on the page.

Yahtzee, he says, when he describes war.
Snake eyes, when he suffers love.
Boxcars, I think as the woman beside me
texts in tattoos and a dog collar,

boxcars rattling down a rusted track
through the darkness of Illinois fields,
past Mattoon, Effingham, and Centralia,
all the way to De Soto and my sister's farm,
where the songs of birds make sense.

Fire, Ice, Latte

Yesterday I was in Atlanta.
Today I am in Chicago sipping
cappuccino at the Atlanta Bread Company,
a bakery and café adjacent
to Borders Books Music and Café,
down the street not far
from Panera Bread, a kind of café
and sandwich spot.

Starbucks looms
and, in its shadow, Caribou Coffee,
not to mention the Cup and Saucer,
a local favorite one block east
of Townhouse Books and Café,
a place that was today
too crowded to eat in.

I worry about all this caffeine
and these baked goods:
triple chocolate chunk cookies,
oatmeal, peanut butter,
white chocolate macadamia,
Bundt cakes and biscotti,
the cinnamon raisin nut rolls.

I wonder about an old farm
outside my table's new window:
the weather-beaten barn,
topless silo standing
still life in a museum
of an undeveloped corner lot.

I wonder if the Atlanta Bread Company
really comes from Atlanta.
The boy at the counter doesn't know.
Good guess, he says and laughs.
He's rushing to make a grande
decaf vanilla chai spiced latte
as if there were no tomorrow.

Station

Not a streetlamp here,
not a house,
not the bright concision of train tracks
leading anywhere else.

There are questions posed
by an owl. There is the dirt
and its memory.
There is the rising and falling of light.

Look up at your map
of the ancient world. Beyond
all land is ocean. Beyond ocean
is the edge.

Suppose there is a god.
That is an order.
Although the question of authority
is moot.

We have our tickets, our destination.
Is this our station,
a nod to some slight preference
for matter?

Magic

Think of a number from one to ten.
Remember that number.
Pick a card, any card.
Slip it back into the deck.
Pick up the dice.
Roll them in your hand.
Blow on them, place them
carefully under one green cup.
Take the deck and cut it.
Place one card face down
on top of each cup.
Put the remainder of the deck
into the top hat.
Pick up the cane.
Tap the hat three times.
Remove three white doves and
put the hat on your head.
Lie on the table.
Secure each manacle
around a wrist or ankle.
Lock them. Don't be afraid
if you glimpse a saw.
Close the box.
When you disappear,
stand up, take a bow.
Accept your bouquets.
Walk proudly from the stage,
past the lights and out
into your vast ovation.

Record High

Yesterday, winter called in sick
and spiked a fever to seventy degrees.
At the airport, where they keep records,
February was delirious.

On the street it tore the tops
from convertibles and the coats
from children as they lingered
outside the open doors at school.

Its own gray coat of clouds
unraveled as it danced
mountain high, spinning to a shirt
of postcard perfect Hawaiian sky.

It must have dreamed of kites
and the kinds of birds that sing
songs that greet a red sun rising
above a coconut tree,

calenture by a tropical sea.
It sweated sheets as it turned
in cramps and windy spasms to fall
freezing beneath a woolen afternoon

but was back on its feet by morning,
whistling like some jaded civil servant,
kicking snow and shaking garbage cans,
rocketing lids through the cold clear air.

Thank You for Calling

The party you wish
to speak to is on the phone.
Is unavailable.
Has stepped away from their
desk.
If you know your party's
extension, you may dial it.
Please press star if you would like
a list of names.
Press pound and the first four letters
of the party's last name. I'm sorry,
S-A-N-D is not a correct
extension.
Press star if you would like a list
of extension numbers.
I'm sorry your party cannot be
reached by this method.
By this method press star
after the tone and your message
will be sent.
If you would like to leave a
message please press pound.
To mark your message
urgent,
press star. Press pound. Press
pound, star, pound.
To confirm your message
in the system
press pound. Pound. Pound.
Pound. Pound. Pound.
Pound.
Or simply hang up. Thank you.
Your message has been
received.

Postmodernism

The cutting edge of poetry
is poised above the poet's wrist.

She has found a million ways
not to say anything.

Not to say there is anything
not to say or anything

else.

Enlightenment

The car ahead is screaming
Coexist! as we slow to a stop.
*Just Because I'm Different
Doesn't Mean I'm Wrong,* it shouts.
I've lowered my gaze.
I don't know why
but I can't stop from looking up to find
*This Car Enjoys Reserved Parking
For Witches,
All Others Will Be Toad.*
I must *Imagine No Religion*
and *Remember That a Mind Is Like
a Parachute,
It Does Not Work If It's Not Open.*
Also *Bigotry
Is Not a Family Value* and *Opinion
Without Information
Is Ignorance.*
I have learned so much,
I cannot be more grateful
to be found in a flash
of transforming green light.
Like St. Paul, I am
struck dumb by the news
that *Dumbledore Is Gay.*

Hold My Beer and Watch This

Immortal words printed on a coaster
given as a gift by a friend
who rode his motorcycle from Illinois
to the northernmost town in Alaska.

Along the way he stopped
for a cold one in Missoula, Montana,
and thought of us as he sipped his Kodiak Pilsner
or Sled Dog Stout or Eskimo Cabbage Pale Ale.

He looked down and found the round reminder
of a time another man once camped
beneath the neon of this same beer sign sky,
maybe after an invigorating hike

through the splendor of Bitterroot Forest
or a fishing trip with Richard Hugo.
This man once bet the guy beside him,
the one in the buffalo-plaid lumberjack shirt,

as they gazed pie-eyed out a back door window
before an audience of empty bottles,
that he could ride that big black bear
sniffing the lid of a dented garbage can.

Aunt Irene at the Piano

There are small, smoky clubs in Hell
where she's in heaven,
three shows a night, no intermission.

After each soul-sucking day
shoveling sulfur, the damned troop in.
They settle at the beer-stained bar

on wooden stools with one leg short.
They order their watered-down shots,
chain-smoke free cigarettes.

At her untuned Steinway Grand,
she caterwauls the length and breadth
of Tin Pan Alley's vaudeville catalogue,

damaging notes and crippling melody
the way disease attacks a host.
It's her regular gig for good,

so to speak, in every dark dive
where the lost lean eternally
toward the door and closing time.

Doodling

I have inked the form
of a crescent moon rampant
upon a marigold field
of legal-pad sky.

There are dinosaurs beneath
or parts of one
or parts of what could be
a dragon.

The fender of an old car,
a Jaguar, something
vaguely English, rests
against the wizened trunk
of a half-imagined cypress tree.

The tip of my pen
is flying there,
from branch to branch
like a nervous bird warning
squirrels from her hidden nest.

I follow it deeper
into the luring leaves,
unfurling themselves beneath
its concupiscent touch,
to the shapes of clouds in the distance,

to the caliphate
of this new Islamic moon
and the dark stars beyond it.
I can feel the sweeping arcs
of my arms curve and lengthen.

As a cross-hatched shadow falls
across my face and shoulders,
this body flows
into the earth of a dozen pages
taking root
where nothing before has grown.

Legal-Ruled, Micro-Perforated, Canary

I love the blue lines.
I love the yellow spaces between
the blue lines.

There are twenty-eight
on each page, bright
as sunbeams

and twenty-nine blue
lines crisp as the creases
on policemen's pants.

The sunbeams are marching
down the page now,
possibility on parade,

and the blue lines,
those cops on the beat,
keep everything moving

nice and neat, and I
watch the waiting boulevard
to see what floats by.

Bathroom Zen

Love the way the cloth says
*cheese*burger, *cheese*burger
as it cleans the glass.

Love the limpid depths of the mirror.

Love the bird whose song
is a rusty gate
and the mysterious fog
in stainless steel.

Love the bug with no name,
the way fresh mud catches a stone.

Love the well-read look
of magazines
as ants might love
a peony.

Love the patient devotion
of the dressing table.

Love the spark, the brassy pride
of polished knobs
like luteous doodles
of fireflies.

Love the fortitude of porcelain.

Love the bright
plumage of a prism on an old tiled wall.
Love it all:

the squeal of the cloth,
the mirror's laughter.

Idyll

We are climbing to our Zen moment.
We are pulling a blanket over our heads.

We are trying to absorb the lessons of clouds.
We are inhabiting the darkness of windows.

We are listening to songs of the Kinks,
lazing on this sunny afternoon.

We are whispering words for the air conditioner,
the desultory charm of a bee.

We are mulling the meaning of timelessness.
We are measuring bricks to the curb.

We are thinking we hear a harmonica
in the great gray distance of memory.

Oh Shenandoah, it plays, *we're bound away
across the wide Missouri.*

Contentment

At the insistence of these salt and
pepper shakers,
at the direction of this table lamp
dressed as an early American
and the checkerboard cloth beneath it,
I am writing.

I have known the succulence
of grilled cheese, the fresh balsamic voice
of a salad. I have sipped my boundless tea
again and again.

Time does not pass so much
as contemplate its own passing
here at the corner of lunch and breakfast
where radio frees the buried soul
of the 1970s.

If lovin' you is wrong,
we don't want to be right.
From the world of everyday light,
the pedestrian send valentines
To Whom It May Concern.

Acknowledgments

Atlanta Review: "Where the Mouse Was," "Old Movies"
Bitter Oleander: "What They Know"
Cider Press Review: "Thirty-four Cranes," "Winter
     Storm," "Seriatim," "Staggered, Stunned by Light"
The Lyric: "Twelfth Moon"
Open Spaces: "Thank You for Calling"
Poetry East: "Two Pots of Begonias"
River Oak Review: "June Bugs"

*Cover artwork, "Philbin Beach Path" by Katherine
Gendreau Photography; cover and interior book design
by Diane Kistner; Cronos Pro text and Arial Black titling*

About FutureCycle Press

FutureCycle Press is an independent press dedicated to publishing lasting English-language poetry books, chapbooks, and anthologies in both print-on-demand and Kindle ebook formats. Founded in 2007 by long-time independent editor/publishers and partners Diane Kistner and Robert S. King, the press incorporated as a nonprofit in 2012. A number of our editors are distinguished poets and writers in their own right, and we have been actively involved in the small press movement going back to the early seventies.

The FutureCycle Poetry Book Prize and honorarium is awarded annually for the best full-length volume of poetry we publish in a calendar year. Introduced in 2013, our Good Works projects are anthologies devoted to issues of universal significance, with all proceeds donated to a related worthy cause. Our Selected Poems series highlights contemporary poets with a substantial body of work to their credit; with this series we strive to resurrect work that has had limited distribution and is now out of print.

We are dedicated to giving all of our authors the care their work deserves, making our catalog the most diverse and distinguished it can be, and paying forward any earnings to fund more great books.

We've learned a few things about independent publishing over the years. We've also evolved a unique, resilient publishing model that allows us to focus mainly on vetting and preserving for posterity poetry collections of exceptional quality without becoming overwhelmed with bookkeeping and mailing, fund-raising activities, or taxing editorial and production "bubbles." To find out more about what we are now doing, come see us at www.futurecycle.org.

The FutureCycle Poetry Book Prize

All full-length volumes of poetry published by FutureCycle Press in a given calendar year are considered for the annual FutureCycle Poetry Book Prize. This allows us to consider each submission on its own merits, outside of the context of a contest. Too, the judges see the finished book, which will have benefitted from the beautiful book design and strong editorial gloss we are famous for.

The book ranked the best in judging is announced as the prize-winner in the subsequent year. There is no fixed monetary award; instead, the winning poet receives an honorarium of 20% of the total net royalties from all poetry books and chapbooks the press sold online in the year the winning book was published. The winner is also accorded the honor of being on the panel of judges for the next year's competition; all judges receive copies of all contending books to keep for their personal library.

www.ingramcontent.com/pod-product-compliance
Lightning Source LLC
Chambersburg PA
CBHW070010100426
42741CB00012B/3179